the
LESSON

Personal Development

Encouraging, Motivating, Inspirational
www.KLETL.com

Published by Krystal Lee Enterprises (KLE Publishing)
Copyright © 2016 by K. Lee All rights reserved.

Printed in the United States of America.

All rights reserved. No part of this book may be reproduced or transmitted in any form or by any means, electronic or mechanical, including photocopying, recording or any information storage and retrieval system without written permission of the publisher except for brief quotations used in reviews, written specifically for inclusion in a newspaper, blog, magazine, or academic paper.

ISBN: 978-0-9971378-6-6
Library Control #2016918198

Book Production: KLE
Cover Design: KLE: Krystal Lee

Paperback:
All rights reserved. Please send comments and questions:
Krystal Lee Enterprises
sales@KLEPub.com

To Reach the Author:
Email: me@authorklee.com

Web: Authorkleecom
Social: IG, FB, Twitter, TikTok, Youtube
@AuthorKLee

Contact: Phone: 770-240-0089
Printed in the United States of America.

Dedication

I trust this book series will encourage all youth and persons that read and utilize this book and the books to come that complete the series. Remember, the youth is the future so invest in them.

Special thanks to: To my Lord and Savior Yahshua (Jesus Christ), Dr. Sharron Cross, Sherrie Raymore, Pamela Mathis, Uche Njoagwuani, Dr. Judith Fletcher, Ms. Yulanda, Bishop William Martin, Dr. W. Michael and Julia Turner, Jaylin Turner.

Chapters:

Foreword.. 7

Introduction.. 11

Blended Families................................. 15

Who are You?..................................... 23

Comfortable In Your Own Skin.............. 35

Create the You, You want to Be 47

Frame of Mind.................................... 57

The Basics.. 67

Rise Above the Bully............................ 87

Leadership 101................................... 95

No One is Perfect 105

About The Author.. 113

Resources 116

The Lesson: Personal Development Author K. Lee

Foreword

We live in a world where every young girl and boy has the choice to decide who he or she is and will become. The Lesson program was created to encourage the boys and girls of today to press toward the mark and not allow limitations, fears, and reservations to cloud their vision, cementing their feet in failure or poor progress.

Our youth are smart, intelligent, and innovative and need possibilities that will encourage their growth. Our children are capable of leading Fortune 500 markets with buying power, developing industries, and being one of the largest sales forces in America. This group can talk their parents, grandparents, and loved

Foreward

ones into purchasing phones, gaming systems, and entertainment that are equivalent to the cost of a monthly car payment, rent payment, or utility bill.

This group must be catered to, if not for the good nature of man, society, and community, but also because they support the US Economy. Every company must understand that this generation will secure their future or be a part of the reason they will report record lows. We want to educate this group to leverage their influence to improve their future, the outlook of their community, and society as a whole.

Young person, you have a right and should enforce your ability to make a difference in this world. You don't have to sing, dance, or act to make an impact in the business landscape. You can cook, create technology, speak, market, promote, teach, create a business, get involved in government, and so much more! Use your age to your benefit and trust in your natural talents. Greatness is in you, and this program is set up to draw it out.

What can you expect from The Lesson? The Lesson book series is a tool for the parent, guardian, mentor, and a guide for the student. The Lesson program encourages youth to get engaged with mentors, their peers, and activities through social media, appearing at bi-weekly events, attending events, and participating in training and career day follow-alongs or internships. We are a hub providing resources, information, and support to encourage the youth to go for their dreams!

You are on the right track to have picked up this

book and started reading it. We challenge you to finish it and get involved with The Lesson Program. Throughout the book, when you see #KLETL, we encourage you to post your thoughts via social media and share in groups.

When you get involved with The Lesson program, we are here every step of the way to provide you with valuable advice in 5 powerful ways: via our book series, TV Show, magazine, website, and app. Completing this book is a great milestone you have accomplished, and The Lesson is here to support you all the way! Don't get discouraged in well doing. Stay focused and passionate about investing in your future.

PASS "The Lesson!"

The limit is beyond the sky!

Foreward

Introduction

This book is intended to be a tool to help today's youth determine who they are and want to become and put plans in place to get them there. The Lesson series is a book series that includes personal development, career exploration, life application, financial empowerment, and assistance for pre-teens and teenagers.

This book can be used as a tool by both the instructor/parent/mentor and the youth. Each book talks about core concepts facing our youth and how they can overcome, maneuver, and succeed in life. By reading this book series and utilizing the information enclosed, our next generation can be focused and concerned

Introduction

about the well-being of themselves and others, as well as develop a global perspective.

This installment of The Lesson focuses on Personal Development. Before you can go out in search of who you want to become, you have to know who you are. What you discover about yourself may not all please you, but you can change, improve, and put practices in place to become the you, you want to be. The following chapters are an introduction to key concepts for evaluating your goals, interests, challenges, successes, and losses. We suggest ways to face hard issues so you are not overwhelmed or feeling defeated.

After you complete this book, we hope you will have a solid understanding of who you are and at least an idea of who you want to become. Completing this book is a milestone, but keep in mind that it is a guide intended to be referenced as much as needed. Be sure to complete the activities and check out other available videos, books, courses, and resources.

K. Lee, a certified and licensed International Transitional Life Coach, writer, and program developer, wrote this book. Krystal is passionate about helping young people reach their fullest potential. Her deep passion for their success also influences her desire to see their parents and loved ones free and able to reach beyond the sky!

The Lesson: Personal Development Author K. Lee

To learn more, visit the following websites or scan the QR codes below:

www.KrystalLeeEnterprises.com
www.KLETL.com
www.AuthorKLee.com
770-240-0089 Ext 0
me@authorklee.com
Social: @AuthorKLee on All platforms

Introduction

The Lesson: Personal Development Author K. Lee

Blended Families

This book series makes no assumption about your family structure. We live in a society with numerous kinds of family structures. As you read this book, we want you to know that your upbringing can impact your life but doesn't dictate where it's going; "You Do!"

Take a moment and try to describe your family structure or upbringing. Who's in your family? Do you have siblings? Who is your primary caregiver? Do you have multiple homes? Do you live with your mother and father? Are your parents married or single? Have you been adopted? My last question is, what does family mean to you?

Blended Families

_____

_____

_____

_____

_____

_____

_____

As you can see, all of our answers will vary from person to person. I was born into a family of five children. My mom was a single parent on and off again, as she married and divorced a few times. I did not grow up in just one city nor attend the same school for all my schooling. I went to several schools and was glad that my High School years were all at one school.

As far as my parents are concerned, I didn't grow up with my mother and father at home. In fact, I never knew my birth father—still don't know him, and I'm 30 writing this book. There were challenges in my life that perhaps knowing my father could have helped me deal with, but I became stronger and now can help others.

I know what it's like to be raised by grandparents because, during summer vacation, I visited my grandparents all the time. My grandmother was a school-

The Lesson: Personal Development Author K. Lee

teacher who later became a dean of a high school and stayed in that position until she retired. My other grandparents were similar in that my other grandmother was also a teacher and taught special education until she retired. I loved being with them and could envy those who were raised by them!

My mom's Grandmother also raised her during her younger years; she has nothing but great stories of her upbringing. There is nothing quite like grandparents! While in school, I had friends who also came from single-parent homes, were raised by their grandparents, and some were adopted. My friends who were adopted or living in a foster home always seemed to make me love and appreciate my mom more.

I remember there was a lady at the top of our street who had about four or five foster children living in her large home. They all were well groomed, ate well, and were super nice. Whenever they came over to my house, my mom would always say how polite and thankful they were and that I should be more like them. I took her advice, and they were great friends to me; I learned a lot from them.

Some families that I do realize exist and want to acknowledge are homes with two moms or two dads, families with two sets of parents living in two different homes, and homes where aunts/uncles/siblings or others are your legal guardians. All these homes may appear different, but most homes want the same thing for their house.

No matter who lives or has lived in your home and who cares for you now, know they all want you to

Blended Families

make it and excel in your dream. Your financial condition doesn't change this fact either. If your parent or primary care person doesn't demonstrate this or say it often, know that's their heart's desire, even if they don't realize it. When you make it and accomplish your dream, they will show up and say this is what they wanted for you all along.

I also want to share that there are different parenting methods, and not all are the best. All parents make mistakes because no one is perfect. Try to understand your caregiver's limitations and see things from their perspective, too. It may be hard or easy for you, but after reading this book, we trust you will be able to empathize.

Some behaviors are never acceptable, and although they may be uncomfortable, they should be written down and shared with someone if you need help. If there is anything that is happening in your home that bothers you, please share that with someone you can trust. You should not be hurting in silence or feel that you are all alone. Other families can often help, teachers, pastors, friends, and others. You can also reach out to an external 1800 helpline that can help 24/7, including holidays, nights, and weekends: 1-800-800-5556

_____

_____

_____

The Lesson: Personal Development Author K. Lee

What are some cases that you should report to a person you trust? If your parent, guardian, or someone in or around your home is touching you inappropriately, talking to you vulgar, beating you with objects, fist fighting you, or forcing you to commit crimes (stealing, beating up people, selling drugs, making drugs, or anything similar).

You do not have to live with nor make excuses for people who make harmful decisions. It is not your fault; you cannot control people and should not protect them. Some people need help with counseling or resources, and yes, some even need jail time to reflect on their choices. Don't rob them of their healing, and don't rob yourself of your freedom. No one should have to live in an abusive situation, period.

No abuse is acceptable, and all abuse should be reported. If you don't feel there is someone you can trust to talk to, call this number: 1-800-799-SAFE (7233) or 1-800-787-3224 (TTY). You can also send an email to The Lesson at info@thelessonprogram.com, and we can help get you to the right people and resources.

We want to see you living well and accomplishing your dreams. It is tough to make it with obstacles in your way. Remove the obstacle, report it, and begin to heal. You can survive and overcome anything because you are more than a conqueror; you are a natural-born leader.

Blended Families

Chapter Recap!

Blended families are a gift to society. Often than not, blended families are the norm. Don't believe for a second that your family condition or financial picture can stunt your growth. You are a natural-born leader, more than a conqueror! Take the time, do the work, and Pass The Lesson!

Great Work So Far!
Let's Get the Ball Rolling!

For Coaching Participants in The Lesson Program
Activity: Write down your assignment and due date!
1.
2.
3.
4.

Notes:

To Enroll, Scan the QR or visit KLETL.com

Blended Families

Who are You?

Who are you? It seems like a simple question, doesn't it? After further consideration, perhaps the question is not so simple. This is a loaded question because there is no simple answer to define you! A loaded question is a question that, when you attempt to answer it, a series of other questions pop up.

Take this for an example: if you are asked, "How was your day?" There is a simple answer you could give, "great," "good", "alright." In your mind, however, a more developed conversation takes place to arrive at this answer. Perhaps the inner dialogue is something like this:

Who Are You

1: What happened today?
2: Did I like what happened today?
3: Did I give my best to solve the problem?
4: Can I live with myself?
5: Do I need to tell anybody?
6: Will I tell anybody?

This series of questions and answers that take place in your mind, more often than not, create your one-word response: "good," "great," "alright," etcetera (etc). Now, consider the question at hand, "Who are you?" What would you say if you could explain who you are in a few words, or max three mini sentences? #KLETL

_____

_____

_____

_____

_____

_____

_____

I am sure you wrote something great to describe who you are! Every person is wonderfully made and equipped with talents, abilities, interests, likes, and dislikes. I have one more quick question I want you to ponder and answer. What do you think "You are who you prove to be" means? #KLETL

_____

_____

_____

_____

Let's talk a little more about this strong statement and discuss your findings. Perhaps some of the situations below will gel with some of your findings about people you know.

1: Has anyone ever told you they were nice, but you see them act cruel or rude more often?
2: Has a person told you they are skinny, and you don't see it?
3: Have you heard a person tell you they are fat, and you don't see how they got to that conclusion?
4: Have you met someone who told you they are smart, but you constantly see them making unsmart decisions?
5: Or perhaps you have heard someone tell you they are good at this or that—now you may think we need to define the word "good!"

Everything a person tells you about him or herself is not always true. If you watch talent search programming on TV or videos online, you could laugh for days at people who don't reach the bar for greatness—but that doesn't mean they can't improve.

Who Are You

The point "good" is subjective to the eye or ear of the beholder—unless there is a standard.

During these competitions, there is always a standard set by the original artist. If the singer can't hit the notes, they crack, or their voice disappears when needed most. You would probably say, "They can't sing" or "They are trying too hard." If the dancer can't keep up or lose track of the beat, they "fail." If an actress is not believable, forgets their lines, or their scene is boring, the audience will say they are "lame."

Some things you may believe about yourself may also not be true. So, let's look back at the word "good." What do you think is meant when someone says, "I am a good person?" Do you believe there is a standard for being good? List 3 to 5 things you think make a good person, and remember to share at #KLETL

_____

_____

_____

_____

Here are the top ten answers we have read. See how your thoughts compare.

1: Listen to your Mother/Father Guardian
2. Do not steal
3: Do not lie (Be honest)
4: Don't be Jealous of others

The Lesson: Personal Development Author K. Lee

5: Don't get envious of others
6: Don't be cruel to others
7: Do not cheat
8: You stick to your personal beliefs
9: You value your word
10: Do not use foul language

Do you agree with the list? Share your list at #KLETL because we would love to hear your thoughts! Also, after looking at the list, do you feel that some of the items listed don't fit who you prove to be? In short, would you say some things on the list that make a good person, you don't do them at all or only sometimes? If you answered "yes," that makes you human! We all strive to be good but are not perfect; we are all a work in progress.

The next question you may have is, how can I master being good? I want you to hold on to that thought as we are going to talk about that in great detail in Chapters 2 through 12. Before we go, there is one more thing I want you to consider. This chapter has a lot to do with what you do to be a good person, but what about what you think? Do you believe what you think impacts what you do—who you are?

I am sure the answer you got to this question is "yes." The things you think about and what you believe about yourself shape who you are and will become. Let's look at a few things you think about or believe are true and see how it impacts who you are. For this quick exercise, there are five categories:

1: Prejudice: Are you prejudiced against people

Who Are You

who are older than you? Do you make fun of people with learning or physical disabilities? Do you dislike people who are of a different race, gender, or sexual preference? Do you treat people who are different from you differently or with the same respect?

Your Notes:

___

___

___

___

2: Are you an optimist or a pessimist? Do you look at life and see all the ways your life can get better throughout the day? Or do you look at life and see all the ways life can move for the worse? If you see life as always being able to improve, get better, and be happier, you are an optimist. If you see life as one click away from going from okay to bad and that the glass is half empty and not full, you would be considered a pessimist.

Your Notes:

___

___

___

The Lesson: Personal Development Author K. Lee

3: Emotions. Would you say you are in charge of your emotions? Do you feel you have control over what's happening in your life? Are you quickly agitated? Do you have tons of patience for people or yourself?

Your Notes:

_____

_____

_____

_____

4: Attitude. Would you say you have a positive attitude? Does your attitude help resolve problems or start them? Does your parent, teacher, or guardian say you have a positive attitude or a negative one?

Your Notes:

_____

_____

_____

_____

5: Body Language. What does your body language say about you? Do your eyes roll when you listen

Who Are You

to instructions? Do you flip your hair and turn when being spoken to, or do you walk away? Do you listen attentively or listen only to retaliate or defend yourself?

Your Notes:

_____

_____

_____

_____

If we are honest, these five categories may reveal not-so-great things about who we are. We may find that we are prejudiced against people because they are different from us. We may have to face the fact that we are pessimists and see life as one click away from disaster instead of having the potential to get better moment after moment. Or perhaps you find that your body language says you are rude and don't care, but you want to care.

If some of these statements are true, if this chapter has revealed more about who you are, you have done the hard work! In the next chapter, we are going to talk about being Comfortable in Your Own Skin. I want to show you how to take your answers and use them to take you to the next step to help you find your comfort zone!

So how can you get to know you? The characteristics you have may determine who you are, but there

The Lesson: Personal Development Author K. Lee

is more to you. Remember, traits and ideas only determine who you are today. You can choose at any time to change your today and impact your tomorrow.

Who Are You

Chapter Recap!

Take a moment and review your answers to the tough questions. If you are comfortable, share your thoughts via the app, in your group, and share your thoughts about this chapter on social media (#KLETL). In the next few chapters, the hard work you put in now will help you transition smoothly from step to step! So take the time, do the work, and Pass The Lesson!

Great WORK!
Keep Pushing to the Finish!

For Coaching Participants in The Lesson Program
Activity: Write down your assignment and due date!
1.
2.
3.
4.

Notes:

To Enroll, Scan the QR or visit KLETL.com

Who Are You

The Lesson: Personal Development Author K. Lee

Comfortable in Your Own Skin

You did fantastic work in the previous chapter. Now, let's take a look at what the work means. Some things you may notice about yourself based on the previous chapter may include shortcomings, a realization that you are not perfect and that your background and family history have contributed to the way you think. All of us have life experiences that help shape the way we think.

One thing I want to point out and will speak about often in this book is bullying. There are bullies out there who may not know they are a bully, and youths who are being bullied may not realize it. We

Comfortable in Your Own Skin

want to talk about this problem because young bullies grow up to be adult bullies. If you are comfortable in your own skin, there is hope for you to appreciate the differences of others. In the previous chapter and throughout the book, you will identify unique differences between you and others.

As you progress through the book and see the value of diversity, you will become more comfortable in your own skin. People, youths who are comfortable in their own skin, don't feel the need to control everyone else around them. This desire not to control other people will help you avoid being/becoming a bully and increase your friendship ability level. Allow me to explain.

In the previous chapter, we discussed how what you do and think, once played out, proves who you are. If you treat people differently because they are not like you, you may be prejudiced. Prejudice is not limited to race but includes gender, financial well-being, age, physical or mental disabilities, body type, physical makeup, and sexual preference or orientation.

What I want you to understand is that you can dislike something, not agree, but be tolerant and respectable to others. Tolerance is not agreement, and agreement shouldn't limit tolerance. You can disagree with someone and still be courteous, thoughtful, and respectable. During your school quest, there will be plenty of subjects where you can share your opinion on a subject, event, or topic. You can discuss a topic, acknowledge an opinion, and express your own.

The Lesson: Personal Development Author K. Lee

Your teacher is not expecting you to agree with everything you learn but to understand it and be able to accurately explain your thoughts and ideas. In expressing your thoughts, you are not expected to force someone to see as you do but have a desire for people to understand you so they can make their own decisions.

This chapter is all about you getting comfortable and familiar with who you are so you can best explain yourself to others. First, I want you to write one sentence that explains who you are. Yup, the previous chapter is at work! #KLETL

_____

_____

_____

Now, I want you to write one sentence on what makes you comfortable with who you are. #KLETL

_____

_____

_____

Lastly, what advice would you give to help someone else be comfortable with who they are? #KLETL

_____

Comfortable in Your Own Skin

_____

_____

Learning who you are is a vital step to becoming comfortable in your own skin. Being comfortable in your own skin doesn't mean you may not want to change anything. It just means you know who you are—you see where you are, and you own your choices. Owning your choices means, if you did the work in chapter one, you discover key attributes that explain your character. You can also acknowledge that those traits and choices are a big part of Chapter 2.

Next, let's take a look at some popular categories for question number two. What makes you comfortable with who you are? There are lots of answers, and clearly no wrong answer to this question. Here are some of the popular answers and takeaways I have to offer.

"When I like me, I am comfortable with who I am." When you like who you are, it is easy to be comfortable with who you are. If you can love yourself, it is easy to love others like you love yourself. If you can see the value in yourself, your differences, and your unique capabilities, you can reflect that energy to others.

In school, there are a lot of crowds. The in-crowd, the out, the smart, etc., there is nothing wrong with finding like-minded people. The second response most often received was, "I am comfortable with who I am when I know I am not the only one." There is comfort in numbers and surely confidence to be you when you know others like you too!

Finding the right friends may sound easy, but it can take time to find the right group for you. Sometimes, finding the right group means leaving your current environment, seeking out activities outside your school, joining clubs, or taking classes. When you get involved with projects, programs, and classes that make you happy, never stop going because of what others have to say.

Everyone is entitled to an opinion, and the most important opinion concerning you is what you think about yourself. You are or will become, who you say and think you are! Speak positively, think positively, and positive things will happen. This may not happen overnight but don't get discouraged. Change takes time, but the time is always well spent!

The third response we've gotten is: "I am comfortable in my own skin when others like me." The desire to fit in is human, and you shouldn't feel guilty about wanting others to like you. One thing you ought to consider is who you want to like you. Again, everyone has an opinion, but whose opinion do you value? Some people value their parents' opinions, teachers, coaches, pastors, friends, or God's, among many others.

But what do you say? Depending on who you are, your answer will vary. If you are an athlete, you may say that my coach is important to me. If you want to be a college graduate, you would probably say your teach-

Comfortable in Your Own Skin

er. Depending on what field you want to enter into as an adult, you would say someone with a well-respected rapport in that industry.

Having a positive role model that you look up to and desire to model your life after is key to helping you make important decisions in life. You all are at a stage where there is a lot about life you don't know. As you grow older, you will realize there is still more you don't know. Don't let this handicap you from moving forward. Try to find a role model to be the springboard for where you want to go.

When you are selecting a role model, there are no limitations or set rules for who you pick. You may choose people or organizations that are famous or just well-known by you. Here is a short list of a few reasons or role model types you may select. The great thing about role models is that you are not limited to having one, not even one per category. You can have as many role models as you prefer. #KLETL

1: Their Character/Attitude
2. Physical Appearance/Fashion
3: Occupation
4: Accomplishments
5: Social Influence
6: Talent/Skill
7: Common Interest

Take a moment and jot down some role models you have in your life. Also, write down why you picked them. Do you like their character, appearance, occupation, skill, etc.? #KLETL

The Lesson: Personal Development Author K. Lee

_____

_____

_____

Now about that helpful advice you gave to encourage others to be comfortable in their own skin. Allow me to share with you my suggestions. There are a few things in life I had to learn to be comfortable with about myself. Growing up, I was not the prettiest or the tallest. I was skinny, I felt my hair braided made me look funny, and I had a lot going on I didn't like. I wasn't a girly girl, and I seemed to fit in nowhere.

I was a middle child, and my mom had five children. I am not sure how she kept up with us, but I wanted to be invisible, so I let my hair go all over the place by the end of the day. I wore the baggiest clothes I could find, and I did this through High School. I was a hot mess and didn't care.

I didn't realize at the time that this seemingly carefree attitude was a cover-up for how I felt about myself. I was uncomfortable and unhappy with who I was. I didn't like myself, and it showed by how I took care of myself, dressed, wore my hair, and even how I talked about myself. I remember one day my mom told me it was not about who my dad was or what I looked like that made me sweet, but my heart.

I remember my teacher, Mrs. Jackson, telling me

Comfortable in Your Own Skin

every student around me would have an opinion, but I only needed to consider what I thought the most. She told me to be sure to value myself. You see, if you don't value who you are, take care of yourself, and protect yourself, no one else will think they have to either! Based on what you put out there, you set the tone for how people see you and what they think about you.

If you want to be known as sweet, kind, happy-go-lucky, well-groomed, and clean, do the things that resonate. You don't want to lose yourself, but lift yourself. Hair, hygiene, and clothes are to adorn who you are on the inside, not hide your inner being. Clothes never make the person, but the person makes the clothes!

I want you to understand that loving you is the first step to valuing ourselves and others. If you don't love yourself, you can't love anyone else. If you don't know how to love yourself, watch how people treat you who truly love you. Prayerfully, we all have a parent, guardian, teacher, pastor, friend, mentor, or sibling who loves us.

Loved people, easily love others because love builds confidence. What is love? Love is patient and kind. It helps you when you are in need, keeps necessary secrets, and gives you honest advice when you need it. Don't turn away from those who love you because they advise you to change this or that, but consider their advice and ask yourself, "Will this make me better? Will I be more comfortable with myself afterward?"

The Lesson: Personal Development Author K. Lee

I took my older sister's advice, and to this day, I take advice from professionals who have a knack for fashion, hair, etc., to help me with my look. When I look good and smell good, I am confident, which makes me feel good. Hygiene and personal upkeep should not be underestimated. The way you care for yourself, do your hair, dress, bathe, use deodorant, and have your smell goods can impact your confidence.

Find the scents you like—the style you want for your hair or fashion. If you don't know, don't be afraid to go to a store and ask! You are in a critical time in your life; put the time in and get comfortable in your own skin.

Comfortable in Your Own Skin

Chapter Recap!

Take a moment and review the questions, discussion, and answers from this session. What were the key takeaways for you? Share them with your group, online or write them below. Remember, loving yourself, being loved, and sharing love is the key to not becoming a bully. Get comfortable in your own skin. Take the time, do the work, and Pass The Lesson!

Great WORK!
Keep Going for the Finish!

For Coaching Participants in The Lesson Program
Activity: Write down your assignment and due date!
1.
2.
3.
4.

Notes:

To Enroll, Scan the QR or visit KLETL.com

Comfortable in Your Own Skin

The Lesson: Personal Development Author K. Lee

Create the You, You Want to Be

I don't know about you, but I didn't come into this world perfectly. I learned to love myself, but I wasn't pleased with everything about myself. To be honest, I was at a loss on how to change myself. Can you relate?

I want you to take a moment and consider this: so far in this book, would you say you are comfortable in your own skin more now than before? Would you say, I know who I am, but I realize I could make some improvements? If you could make improvements, where would you want them? #KLETL

Create the You, You Want to Be

___

___

___

Let's dive a little deeper. First, there is nothing wrong with wanting to improve you. Desiring to improve the you, you are today by making changes is continuing a journey toward a solid foundational pattern for self-improvement. During your life, you are going to always desire to improve the you, you can be. You can improve yourself through education, re-associating yourself in different groups, and trying new things to improve your character, technique, etc.

In a previous chapter, we talked about mentors; now, I want you to consider the mentors you picked. If you haven't selected any yet, let's get that done! In this chapter, we are going to look at the you, you want to become. So, if you could write down how the ideal you would think, look, talk, etc, what would you say? #KLETL

___

___

___

___

I am sure this was a loaded answer for many of

you. If it wasn't, no pressure, you can always come back to this section and add more. I want to share my answer and perhaps it can help shed some light for you. I will break up my mentors into the following sections because I really do have a lot of mentors.

1. Lifestyle/Personal Attitude
2. Occupation
3. Belief System
4. Community Involvement
5. Skills
6. Entertainment

Real quickly, you can select a mentor based on any characteristic you like about a person, organization, or skill. Ideally, your mentor will be a person you want to emulate, so more than likely, they would have mastered something. Okay, who are my mentors, and why did I select them?

The first category is lifestyle and personal attitude. When I was growing up, I was a sweet person, but upon further analysis, I was a passive person. I didn't care about anything; nothing bothered me, and everything in my life was just "blah."

It wasn't until I was in school that I truly discovered kindness. It's funny at home, you figure everyone should be nice to you and vice versa, but at school, you learn it is by choice people are nice to you and vice versa. So, as I started to see many people not befriend me, and perhaps I was shy, I saw a girl in the class who had tons of friends.

Create the You, You Want to Be

I didn't say much, but I watched what she did. To be helpful, she helped people with their homework, sharpened pencils for the teacher, and cleaned up after parties. Some called her names "teacher's pet" and things like that, but I thought she was "sweet."

It was then I understood; I wanted to be like her. Keep this in mind: my first mentor was a peer, so don't discount the peer mentors around you! Toddlers prove how much kids can learn by watching each other. Quick question: what are the peers around you teaching you? #KLETL

_____

_____

_____

Next question, do you need to change your friends? If you become what you take in, take my advice, get new friends, and create new environments that align to get your desired outcome. Now, in the present day, one of my personality mentors is my mom. I chose her because, in her life, she is honest, cares about others, and is not perfect but owns up to her flaws. She is always willing to be helpful. A good mentor doesn't have to be perfect but true to who they say they are.

I am interested in several occupations, but one I want to share here is publishing. I have had the opportunity to meet a handful of publishers personally, and I still believe I have so much more room to grow.

The Lesson: Personal Development Author K. Lee

However, a lady who has inspired my interest is Myrna Gayle of 3G Publishing.

Myrna is a passionate woman with a heart for children. Many of her projects involve working with children and youth to help them get their works published or just put together. Seeing her company grow from a baby to where it's headed is an amazing journey. I look up to her personally, as she is a beautiful soul and a great friend.

My belief system is a cornerstone of my life. Without it, many of the ideals, dreams, and self-love I have now would have been diluted. Three people have been inspirational in my life as it pertains to my personal beliefs: my now-deceased father figure, William "Billy" Hall, and the Turners.

Growing up, I didn't know my birth father. It bothered me for a long time, although I wanted it not to. I tried to get along without a father figure or think stepdads were enough, but it wasn't at the time. I wanted to be normal. I wanted my mom and my dad.

I never got that, but I got something better, I believe. I had several father and mother figures in my life who taught me lessons no two people could have taught me on their own. I learned from Billy that it was never about the man who gave me life but about the people who helped me live life! Billy inspired me to think higher and better about myself. I love him and miss him still.

The Turners are a husband-and-wife couple who

Create the You, You Want to Be

are senior pastors at Kingdom of God Ministries International in Atlanta, GA. This duo has opened their lives, given their time, and extended their home to people in need. I have met a lot of people who hide behind titles, but when you look at their lives, no religion can support their actions.

I love what Dr. Turner said to me one day he said: "Compassion with no action is not compassion at all." One thing about a great mentor is they say what they mean, and they mean what they say. People can make mistakes, but character speaks louder than anything.

He and Mrs. Julia reminded me it is not enough to just say how I feel if I am not going to do anything about it. I'm passionate about youth, empowerment, and helping others, so I started pushing "The Lesson" even more! What about you? Is there anything that bothers you or moves you with compassion? What are you going to do about it? Mentors should motivate you to do more than you thought you could. #KLETL

_____

_____

_____

_____

_____

A community mentor that I think is an incredible example—again, not perfect, is Judge Mathis.

The Lesson: Personal Development Author K. Lee

Judge Mathis is not shy about his past and heart for the future. Judge Mathis had a rough beginning, making bad decisions in the streets, but his mom never gave up on him. She believed in him, and after her passing, Judge Mathis had to believe in himself.

He turned away from a life of crime and poor decisions to fight for his position in the judicial system. He brings his wisdom, compassion, and heart into his courtroom and his community. Judge Mathis built a community center to serve people in Detroit and to give back to people who are walking in his old shoes to redemption.

A mentor list would be incomplete if you didn't like someone because they are skilled in something you do or would like to do. I love to watch cooking shows and to be honest, I am not the best cook in the world. Bobby Flay is one of my mentors for his sheer ability to cook anything and make it look yummy on tv. I went to his restaurant once in Vegas, and it was an "ok" burger. Next time, I want to try one of his dishes, not a burger spot.

I think Bobby is not only a good chief but also a funny one. He has several TV programs, stores, and streams of income. I admire his business sense the most! I haven't learned all the techniques the contestants of Worst Cook in America had to learn, but perhaps someday I could compete. I have come a long way in the kitchen, but I think most of my cooking is a bit average compared to Bobby Flay, and I am okay with that.

Create the You, You Want to Be

My final mentor, whom I wanted to share with you, is in the entertainment industry. Like you, I am very involved in music and movies. One of my top mentors for film is Luc Besson. Studying his films in school and watching several of his films made me like him in High School. I love The Fifth Element, and I think it's cool that he brought sci-fi, comedy, action, and drama under one roof.

My latest vocal inspirations are Jordan Smith from The Voice, Kevin Ross, Maurette Brown Clark, Melvin Crispell, and Maroon Five. My inspirations are quite varied, but I enjoy all kinds of genres. Music can be impactful no matter the style when you enjoy the words or the singing capabilities of the talent. What I love about all of these artists, in addition to their voices, is how they try to be a beacon of positivity and encouragement for people.

Consider your role models and how they influence you. Do they make you push harder for your goals? Give you strength for your journey. If they don't or it's not enough, consider expanding and editing your list.

Chapter Recap!

Becoming the you, you want to become is not decided on a whim. You should select people, organizations, and occupations that move you or inspire you to become greater. Be sure you find your mentors. Also, don't be afraid to update the list and add more! Remember, take the time, do the work, and Pass The Lesson!

Great WORK!
Let's Keep it Going to the Finish!

For Coaching Participants in The Lesson Program
Activity: Write down your assignment and due date!
1.
2.
3.
4.

Notes:

To Enroll, Scan the QR or visit KLETL.com

Create the You, You Want to Be

The Lesson: Personal Development Author K. Lee

Frame of Mind

Becoming the you, you want to become may mean you have to change some of the ways you process information, or at the least change how you think! There are several ways you can change how you process information and what you choose to believe. Here are a few points I want to discuss, and if you have ideas, be sure to capture them within the notes sections. Also, don't be shy; share your ideas with your group on the app or start a conversation online with #KLETL.

1. Books/E-Books
2. Music

Frame of Mind

3. Entertainment
4. Training/School

Everyone should have a personal library in their stash. Regardless of whether your library is physical or virtual, you want to have books that can help you! Congratulations, if you have this book, you have at least one. What books should you read? How often should you read? Why should you read? Maybe some questions you ask.

Why should you read? You should read **one** to increase your vocabulary, **two** to increase your knowledge, and **three** for fun. Reading is truly fundamental, and reading challenges your mind. When you read a book, often at this stage in life, there are few to no pictures. So, you have to rely heavily on your imagination to paint the mental picture of events.

Vocabulary: everyone desires to speak intelligently and effectively in conversation. The best way to improve how you communicate is to read books that are written well. There are phrases, syntax structures, and ways to communicate that you can glean from reading. Often, the way you speak isn't the way you write, but the way you write is better than you speak!

There are a few more benefits of reading that you should also be mindful of. By reading, you learn patience. It doesn't matter how fast or slow you read. Reading usually takes more time than talking. Your memory is also greatly improved by reading because you have to retain what you have read to keep up with the story. Being an expert in comprehension and memory also makes you a great listener.

Being a good listener will encourage people to want to speak to you. Reading books by experts will increase your knowledge, making you the best person to talk to. If you are like most, a million things go through your mind, or there are a million things you can do. When you take the time to sit down and read, you have to focus.

What I like about reading is that it's self-paced, to your leisure, and you can always re-read anything you have read. If you can't speak to someone you admire, it is a great idea to read material from them to glean that understanding. The next question you may have is how often should you read. The time span may vary from person to person, but everyone would agree that reading daily is ideal.

What you should read is a loaded question. You can read about anything and everything. I would give the base that if you have any questions, find popular books by accredited authors on that subject and read them. Accreditation can be obtained by their experience personally, professionally, or vicarious. Vicarious means you learn through another person's experience. The concept of reading is vicarious!

There are a few subjects I recommend any teen read and that includes biographies, memoirs, how-to books, self-improvement techniques, spiritual improvement books, and works for entertainment. Entertainment books fall into drama, sci-fi, novel, action, thriller, etc. A spiritual book can be the Bible, instructional help from divinity professionals, or other similar

Frame of Mind

works. A good goal to strive for is to read a book a month and change up your book category if you like.

Jot down some of the book categories and subjects you are interested in, then make a point to seek out books/e-books containing the information. You may find that some subjects may also have app programs that you can download to your phone to access reading material as well. I personally use a Bible app to make sure I keep up with my daily reading. So, whatever works for you, find your groove and get reading. #KLETL

_____

_____

_____

Okay, we are through with books, let's talk about music. Several different kinds of music exist in the world. There are the standard genres, hybrids, and music that's just in a class all of its own. Why is music important to framing your mind? Because what you listen to, does play a part in shaping your ideas.

What you listen to is like what you eat. Whatever that is, that's what you will become. So, a question I have for you is, "What do you listen to?" What are some of the subjects that reoccur or are emphasized throughout that song or genre? Take a moment, think about it, and jot it down. #KLETL

_____

The Lesson: Personal Development Author K. Lee

_____

_____

Now, looking over the list, how do you feel about the songs you listen to on a common basis? Do you feel the music you listen to is leading you to become a better person, improving your frame of mind to align with your goals? Or do you feel your music selection, topics, and genre don't match the frame of mind you want to have?

Several times in my life I had to revamp my music selection because I desired to change my frame of mind. No genre to me is bad, as much as what is communicated through song may not align with my personal frame of mind. For example, I believe all children have value.

I believe young girls, adult women, and my aunt and grandma have value. So, I don't listen to music that demeans my character or the character of my sisters, friends, and loved ones. I believe if you listen to music long enough that belittles people, you intentionally or unintentionally adopt those thoughts.

Years ago, I may be dating myself, but when I was growing up, it was completely horrible and insulting to call a woman a female dog. If you said it, you were instantly corrected, either in a nice way or sometimes violent way. In today's society, if you turn on your radio or listen to conversations, you hear the word thrown around like a term of endearment. This is

Frame of Mind

largely because people have become numb to the insult and now have engrafted the word into their culture as acceptable.

Music plays a part in what you deem acceptable. Music is more than a beat or rhyme. It is a form of repetition and subliminal training. If you hear "you are smart" and descriptions of how and why in every song you listen to, it will impact your thinking. Hour after hour, you will learn the song lyrics and the beat. You'll sing it aloud or speak those lyrics over your life, not knowing how it will impact you or your relationships.

Positive people tend to have positive things happen to them. People who speak negatively frequently have a negative report. I want to give you the advice to hang around positive people, but don't forget to incorporate positive music into your life. Don't allow negative energy to enter your life based on the music you listen to. Remember, for every beat you like, you can find lyrics to match what you like.

Our last category that can help you shape your mind is entertainment. Entertainment is an open door for interpretation, which could be movies, plays, sports, food, shopping, and so much more! What I would like to learn from you is what do you consider entertainment? #KLETL

The Lesson: Personal Development Author K. Lee

Movies are a big source of entertainment for me. I have personal favorites and genres that are my preference. I also have genres I stay away from because I don't like how they impact my frame of mind. When I was younger, I tried to watch horror movies, and my dreams afterward were horrible. Perhaps you have noticed the same thing?

Another reason I stopped watching horror movies was that they negatively affected my nerves. I would be jumpy and nervous to be alone, and simple noises seemed to startle me. After I gave up horror pictures, those uneasy feelings and fears went away. But perhaps horror pictures aren't the genre you stay away from; maybe it is drama?

I know tons of people who do not like drama in their personal life or in their movies. I can understand their reasoning, "I don't want problem after problem in my life," or "I don't like crying in movies." No matter the genre you like or dislike, ask yourself, how does this film make me feel, encourages me to think, and does it reflect my desired character?

In my opinion, many reality TV programs are not great examples for real life or shaping your frame of mind. Many reality TV stars are famous for being unorthodox, violent, mouthy, or using foul language. This genre seems to ooze drama and conflict without offering positive resolution options.

You have to be careful about what you watch because you will find yourself thinking like them, talking like them, and dressing like them. These characters become your mentors! Now, it may be humorous to watch content that is unbeneficial to your frame of mind a few times, but when it is habitual, it creates habits. If you don't desire to swear or want to stop cursing, it's highly advised to stay away from people and sources where that is the norm.

If you don't want to embrace a frame of mind that is projected by a movie you are watching, don't watch it. If you desire to be celibate, don't watch movies that are borderline pornographic. Consider the frame of mind you want, and protect it by engaging in healthy entertainment options.

I know that not watching or listening to what's popular may make you feel like an outcast. I want to encourage you that there is a world of people like you. Krystal Lee Enterprises produces programming—The Lesson, music, and entertainment for people like you! If you would like to participate in The Lesson Docu-series or book project, scan the QR code to learn more!

Chapter Recap!

Watch what your eyes see, your ears hear, and your body engages in. Be careful about what you expose yourself to frequently because habits are hard to break. You've done the work of designing the better you; don't throw your work down the drain with these sneaky setbacks! Remember, take the time, do the work, and Pass The Lesson!

Great WORK!
Keep Pressing to the Finish!

For Coaching Participants in The Lesson Program
Activity: Write down your assignment and due date!
1.
2.
3.
4.

Notes:

To Enroll, Scan the QR or visit KLETL.com

Frame of Mind

The Basics

Great news—you have completed more than half of the book! Now is a great time to discuss a subject that every teen should read and practice: personal hygiene and health. Young women and men have physical differences, which in turn lead to hygiene differences. In this chapter, we will discuss the basic needs of general and personal health.

As a disclaimer, this book does not discuss the subject of transgenderism. This book does classify young women and young men based on their gender at birth and natural occurrences under such cases. This is to no offense to those who elect a different gender, but the items shared in this chapter are biological

The Basics

discussions and may not be relevant to those who elect a different gender based on social choices and not biological ones.

To start, we are going to discuss skills and techniques every teen should know and then discuss matters relevant to each gender. The three subjects are cooking, cleaning/chores, and personal care. Cooking is a skill that is rapidly fading away in modern society, and that pattern must change.

Learning to cook and prepare meals is absolutely vital to your health, nutrition, and well-being. Learning to cook will allow you to be self-sufficient as a teen and a capable adult. Depending on your long-term goals, if having a family is ideal, you want to learn to cook because eating out will be very expensive and drastically impact your health.

Now, what should you learn to cook? The health pyramid has five categories that offer recommendations for how many vegetables, fruits, proteins/meats, and grains you should eat daily to have a well-balanced diet. Let's talk about how to make these seemingly unrealistic requirements possible.

Ideally, there are three meals in a day, with room to snack in between. The best thing any parent/guardian can do to help their teen/preteen maintain a balanced diet is to plan their meals. Meal planning saves on the grocery bill, eliminates waste, and sets a healthy routine.

Meal plans vary, from talking about the type of

dish to suggesting the exact meal. Having dishes that offer variety is ideal because it eliminates boredom and allows you to incorporate other ingredients that help your health. Here are a few standard meal options, snack ideas, and drinks you can incorporate to keep you on track for daily recommended food groups.

In today's society, we must acknowledge that there are many different eating habits and diets, so don't be afraid to make changes to your routine to fit. If you eat an alkaline diet, vegetarian, gluten-free, etc., simply find what works for you, but make a plan for each day as much as possible to be sure your teen/pre-teen can help you. Help them!

Breakfast is an important meal of the day, but not everyone is a big fan. There are options for those that don't care for breakfast and those that do. A simple breakfast can consist of eating at least one fruit, one grain, one protein, and dairy. A meal may look something like this:

Grain: Toast, Pancakes, Waffles, Crepes, Bagels, Muffin, Oatmeal, Granola Bar, etc.
Fruit: Apple, Peaches, Grapes, Strawberries, Pear, Grapefruit, Orange, etc.
Protein: Sausage, Bacon, Eggs, Drinks, Avocado, Granola Bar, etc.
Dairy: Milk-Nuts/Cow/Goat, Egg, Cheese, Yogurt, Butter, etc.

If you prefer a light breakfast consider a smoothie with fruit and vegetables, a granola bar, cereal, toast/bagels with a spread, flavored breads, or yogurt with

The Basics

fruit and oats. Of course every meal and throughout the day you should drink water. As you can see, you can switch up breakfast every day to make it fun as well as work with your time.

For lunch, there are at least five dishes you can learn to make, and you won't starve if you have to cook for yourself and others. One of the best things about cooking is you can invent new ideas to fit your liking. If you can learn to cook pasta, at least one meat or protein, and cut vegetables, you are on your way. Here are the basics of making lunch.

You can make a salad. Salads are super easy, take very little time, and you can eat the leftovers later at dinner. The key is not to put the dressing on the entire salad, because when you do, what you save can become soggy. For salads, you can add anything you have in the house and that you like. The more vegetables the better and you can also add protein! I recommend getting at least 3 veggies during lunch because you only need two at dinner.

You can make a pizza. Pizza can easily contain three vegetables, dairy items, and a grain. If you haven't made a homemade pizza, you should try it. It is fun and simple; you can also buy the dough or crust premade. All there is left to do is put on the sauce and pick your toppings.

A deli sandwich is a super easy meal and a great way to check off sections on the food pyramid. To make a sandwich, you simply choose a protein if you want it, use a grain, and add your veggies. A sandwich can be made low-carb by substituting lettuce for the bread.

Another super easy meal to make that can keep you full for lunch is soup and grilled cheese. In your grocery store, you can find any kind of soup, creamy, traditional, with meat or tofu, and so much more. If you want a hardy soup you can add rice to your meal. With rice, simply get a rice cooker, put in the right measurements and the gadget does the rest.

An easy dish everyone could learn to make or simply eat is a salsa dip base dish. These dips can have seafood (cold or hot), beans, veggies, or fruit. Typically, the dip is served with toast, crackers, or chips. Often, these dips can be purchased from the store premade, so there is hardly any cooking.

As you become more comfortable with cooking, you can diversify your menu and add more complex foods. I also recommend checking out online recipes and cookbooks or watching cooking shows you like. Some shows are more for entertainment, but there is still a lot you can learn. Don't be afraid to try new foods and learn new things.

Dinner is a meal that you can easily eat items from the lunch or breakfast menu if you are not comfortable cooking. If you can cook meat, veggies, or pasta to temperature, you can make anything. With pasta, you boil it in water with salt, pick a sauce, add veggies, and top it off with cheese—done! You can boil or sauté veggies. Cooking items to temperature may take multiple tries, but don't give up; get better each time. If you want the most nutritional value from veggies, steam them instead of putting them on direct heat in a skillet.

When cooking meat, you want to be sure to cook it properly and to your taste. When learning to cook meat, I recommend you get one-on-one training with an adult. Undercooking certain meats is a huge health risk you do not want to take. If you don't have an adult who can show you, consider taking a class or YouTube it. Having a thermometer also helps you know what temperature your meat is cooked to.

Cleaning and chores are equally important tasks all teens should strive to master. Currently, you reside with an adult entrusted to upkeep your home. In case you feel like your room belongs to you, and you can keep it any way you like. Consider that your parents (or guardian) are expected to ensure you have food, clothes, a room, bed, utilities, etc. By providing these items, do you think it is reasonable for them to tell you how to keep your room? It may seem like a no-brainer to you that your parent or guardian provides such things, and understandably, it is, but there is responsibility extended to you also.

Caring for a teen carries responsibility and so does being a teen. As you grow, your parents are going to entrust you with more responsibility so that you can learn how to someday live on your own. When you start to have responsibility that is a clear sign that your parents acknowledge your growth and want to improve the adult you will soon become.

Don't be angry or frustrated with correction. The

The Lesson: Personal Development Author K. Lee

people in your life that are responsible for you care about your upbringing. There is a way and a better way to do anything; choose to learn the better way!

Parents, guardians, teachers, and similar people are here to help you maneuver through life, avoiding unnecessary pitfalls along the way. So if they instruct you to do something, even though you may think it is dumb, do it first. Then, after you have done it, if you have a better way of doing it, talk to them about it. Great parents are great listeners; they may not agree, but at least you will be heard and can get feedback.

In life, someday, you will have to get a job. At this job, you may have a great idea of how to improve the time, quality, or service that you suggest to your boss. They may decline to implement your recommendations and tell you to continue doing it as told to you. Perhaps your idea wasn't as well thought out, and he/she will point that out, but work to improve your idea. Or, if the idea is right, keep your idea and take it elsewhere, where it would be appreciated.

Have you ever felt that your idea wasn't taken into account? Later on, was it used? How did that make you feel? What did you do about it?

_____

_____

_____

If your advice doesn't work now, it doesn't mean

The Basics

you throw it away but see how you can improve it and implement it elsewhere. Learning to follow instructions and directions and not buck at a system set up to protect you is paramount to your learning process. When you learn to follow instructions and keep an eye out for improvement, you will be super successful in life.

If you are keen on breaking the rules or not following directions, you probably should understand why the rules exist in the first place. Has your parent ever told you not to do that, and you do it, later to find out through pain why you shouldn't have?

I remember when I was a kid, my mom told me not to play with fire, the stove, etc. One day, while she wasn't looking, my siblings and I decided to pick up a plastic fork and put it on the stove to see if it would catch fire or just melt. Well, we found not only did the fork melt, but also it caught fire!

The flame was a lot bigger than we expected and my sister who was holding it dropped it on the floor to stomp it out. In the process, she singed her knee. To this day she has a bubble on her knee for where she was burned to remind her, and us all, not to play with the stove.

I can also tell you about a time when the same sister was told to put her seatbelt on. Again, she didn't do it. We drove down the street a few blocks, not realizing her door wasn't closed all the way. My sister leaned on the door, and it instantly popped open while we were driving! My sister fell out the door, and thank

The Lesson: Personal Development Author K. Lee

God we grabbed her and pulled her into the car before she hit the street!

Lesson: don't play with fire, wear your seatbelt, and follow the rules because they were put in place to protect you. It may not seem that way to you now, but later, you will appreciate it. For example, if you are learning to keep a clean house, you will learn to make up beds, wash clothes, and wash dishes. When you go to college or move out, you can implement the learned behaviors to take care of yourself.

If you keep an unclean house/apartment you will have bugs living with you! You would also have friends who won't come over or eat your food. You don't want to be a slob, it limits who befriends you, will date, like, or marry you!

The final thought about chores, cleaning, and responsibility: learn it now, use it now, and use it later. Now, let's talk a little about personal hygiene. Young ladies and young men alike must learn the basics of proper personal hygiene. At this stage in the game, many of you have physically started or are undergoing lots of changes moving into your teenage and young adult years.

Here are some general personal hygiene requirements before we talk about the gender-specific demands.

Brush Your Teeth Daily. Brushing your teeth regularly and flossing keeps your teeth in good health; it also maintains good smelling breath. If you are out and

The Basics

about, be sure to keep peppermints or gum to keep fresh breath all day. The only thing worse than speaking to someone with sour breath is being picked on for it. You should brush twice daily.

Oh, and properly dispose of gum. Wrap it up and toss it into the trash; please don't stick it on surfaces. I am very pro mints over gum because of the ingredients and what gum can do to your organs and jawline. So do a little research and see which is best for you.

Wash your face daily. Washing your face daily will help to prevent pimples, blackheads, and whiteheads. If you sweat a lot, or if you have oily skin, your face attracts a lot of dirt, and sweat traps it. Help your body fight dirt and wash your face daily. Also, find a good cleanser that works well with your skin. Body soap may not be the best soap for your face. So be sure to experiment with what works best for you, considering the skin sensitivity of your face.

LADIES FIRST, we are going to talk about the ladies, so boys feel free to turn to page 81. During your pre-teen, teen, and years of adulthood, there are some best practices you should know to limit health risks and control body odors. Let's talk about key areas for a girl, and if you have questions, be sure to jot them down.

Menstruation: Every girl/woman in her lifetime will have a menstruation. A menstruation is also known as a period and Aunt Flow. Select the term you are most comfortable with, and let's talk about it.

The Lesson: Personal Development Author K. Lee

A period is normal vaginal bleeding that occurs as part of a girl's/woman's monthly cycle. Every month, your body prepares for pregnancy. If no pregnancy occurs, the uterus, or womb, sheds its lining. The menstrual blood is partly blood and partly tissue from inside the uterus.

I know that was a lot of information and perhaps may sound scary. Don't fear the changes your body is going through or will. Having your period is not embarrassing, nor should it make you feel "icky" or anything similar. A period is natural and happens to all women.

There are two ways to care for menstruation properly. You can choose to wear pads or use tampons. The directions for the use of these products are on the box. If you are unsure how to use them, you can ask an adult, your school nurse, or a woman you are comfortable speaking with openly. In short, if you choose to use pads or tampons, you want to follow the directions on how frequently to change them.

As your cycle progresses, you also want to reduce the size of your pad/tampon to ensure comfort. If you want to keep the area as clean as possible, be sure to bathe/shower during your cycle. Because your period may be new to you, I recommend not wearing light colors until you get comfortable with how frequently you need to change out your pad/tampon. There is nothing more shocking than having an accident in public.

Wiping: As a girl, there are specific directions

for how to wipe after using the restroom to ensure you are keeping your vaginal area clean. All girls/women are encouraged to wipe front to back. This means you should start wiping from your vaginal area and end with your butt. If you go from back to front, you can bring bacteria from your rectum area to your vagina. You don't want to do this.

Bathing: Every teen should make it a habit to bathe/shower once a day and at least once every other day. Women secret vaginal discharge that is normal and sweat in many places that generate odors. You do not want these smells to compound.

Another critical care is wearing deodorant. I do suggest using aluminum-free deodorant because of health factors. If you can't wear deodorant, you can find other organic solutions, like baking soda or something you may make at home using a recipe. In the next section, we discuss hair, and as you grow hair, deodorant is a vital way to control armpit odor. Powder is also a great way to control body or armpit odor because it traps sweat.

Hair: The hair on your head is great, but as you mature, your hair will grow in many more places. Hair may grow under your arms, on your neck, face, legs, arms, belly, and vagina. Depending on your parents, you may or may not be able to shave. Regardless of whether you can or not, it is important to bathe because hair brings heat. The more hair on your body, the higher your chances to sweat.

If you can shave, the frequency of your shaving

The Lesson: Personal Development Author K. Lee

will depend on your body. Normally, you will have to shave once to twice a week, and once you start, you want to continue because hair grows thicker after you shave it. To shave, you want to keep the razor at a slant and be sure not to press the razor to your skin. A razor is already sharp and will cut any hair in its way.

Another option that is a bit more painful than shaving is waxing. Waxing is when you apply wax to your skin, place a strip of cloth over the area, and snatch it off quickly. This method is effective, but yes, it does hurt. After waxing, over time, the pain dulls down, can be faster than shaving, and lasts longer.

The last method to remove unwanted hair is tweezing. If you often have a few stray hairs or want to maintain your eyebrows, you either tweeze or wax them. Shaving eyebrows is not the best way to maintain them, beauty professionals claim, but it is up to you!

I personally have my eyebrows threaded into shape, then have to tweeze any missed hairs after. Threading is when a technician uses thread to pull your hair instead of tweezers. It can be painful when you start, but over time it hurts less. Waxing may be the fastest way of the three.

Again, after doing it often, the pain dulls, and the process is bearable. I started shaving them until I got the courage, so don't feel ashamed if you start/stay with that method.

Clothing: As your body is maturing, clothes

The Basics

don't fit like they used to, do they? As a growing young lady, you want to be sure your clothes fit you and don't squeeze yourself to death. Depending on your home, you may have restrictions on lengths for shorts and skirts. Also, the school system may have restrictions.

I support these restrictions as there is nothing more embarrassing than a young girl falling and everybody seeing everything. Similarly, if you have to bend down to get something or are sitting at your desk, students in the class should not be able to describe your underwear. Prayerfully, they are clean if they are ever accidentally seen.

Something to note: There are also predators that will look at young girls and not know their age. Worse, they may not care because of how a young girl dresses. So be aware of your surroundings and mindful of how you dress for protection.

As girls, you also want to be leery of tight clothing because it can cause yeast infections and generate sweat, which can produce more body odor. Yeast infections are caused not only by clothing but also by other conditions related to hygiene and even pregnancy (this is not an exhaustive list). However, tight clothing increases your chances because tight clothes prohibit air from circulating in your vaginal region.

Whew, we made it through some of the tough conversations, but I am sure you may have additional questions. Please take the time to write down any questions you have. Then, be sure to share your questions with a mentor, parent, guardian, or person you trust.

The Lesson: Personal Development Author K. Lee

There is no such thing as a dumb question. All this is new to you, so be patient with yourself as you work to figure it out.

_____

_____

_____

_____

NOW FOR THE GENTLEMEN, in this section, we are going to discuss some key differences and upkeep you want to manage.

Bathing: All young men are going through major transformations in their teen years. All the running, playing sports, or just walking around you do regularly may now cause you to sweat. To maintain body odor, you must shower/bathe at least once daily. At this age, it is highly recommended that you wear deodorant to trap and control sweat odors as well. Another cool factor you can add to your grooming is buying cologne. Find the right scent for your look and style so you look good and smell good.

Hair: Hair will now start growing in more places than your head. Body hair growth will vary by person, so don't feel embarrassed if your hair grows fast or slow. With some practice, you can maintain the look that works out best for you. Some styles you may not be able to have because of your body type, so find another one you can do. Facial hair is probably the most noticeable

The Basics

of all hair besides what grows on your head. Don't let your growth pattern discourage your confidence.

If you don't have a beard, it is not a sign of slow maturity. In fact, many men go for a clean look, which is shaving off all their facial hair. So you are one step ahead of the game. For those that do have a little or a lot of hair, you want to decide if you like it. If you don't want the hair, you want to look for safe ways to groom and maintain it. The simplest way is to shave, and of course, there are several shaving tools.

If you are comfortable with shaving, you can try shaving with supervision, which is highly recommended for the first few times. If you currently go to a barber, you can consider having them shave it or groom it for you. There are several styles you can cut facial hair into to find your look. Don't be afraid to try a new cut, and remember, it will always grow back. It just may take some time.

To talk about facial hair and ignore the hair on your head would be a mistake. It is recommended that you wash and cut your hair as needed. Depending on your hair demands and desired style, you may also elect to have a barber that keeps you looking good. Most guys I know go to the barber every other week or at least once a month.

Another area where you grow hair that impacts hygiene is in your groin, on your chest, and on your armpits. It is imperative that you shower regularly and don't wear the same boxers, undershirt, or socks two and three days in a row. These three key areas hold

The Lesson: Personal Development Author K. Lee

sweat, pack smells, and will not have you in public with confidence. Remember to wear roll-on deodorant, and try the kind that has a cologne inset for the extra boost of confidence and protection if you like. If you are allergic to a deodorant, try to find an alumnimum-free deodorant.

If deodorant causes your skin to peel, burn, or become irritated, you may have an allergy to its ingredients. Try a different deodorant that is more suited to sensitive skin and keeps you fresh. It can take several attempts to pick the right one for you, so be patient as you try them out.

Grooming: We've covered many of the critical areas; the lighter side of things is to be sure you care about how you dress. Before you leave out each day, make sure you are not wrinkled, your clothes are clean/look clean, and smell clean. A fresh pair of socks and regular washing will keep your shoes from smelling. Washing them and using foot powder are also advised to control sweat. If you wash and take care of what you have by using your shoes and clothes for designated tasks, you will extend the life of your items.

Voice: The last change you will undergo during your journey to adulthood is your voice change. Don't be embarrassed; it is a right of passage for all young men. During this phase, it can be a bit embarrassing if your voice changes at inconvenient times. Don't be too hard on yourself, and remember it will pass. Soon, you will have a voice that fits you just right.

The Basics

Chapter Recap!

Wow, we made it through the longest chapter in the book! Personal upkeep and locking in the basics will be the foundation for your adult life. Don't underestimate these lessons. Listen to your parents/guardians/elders, bathe, brush your teeth, and wash your face daily. Also, learn to cook a little something! Remember, take the time, do the work, and Pass The Lesson!

Great WORK!
I Can Almost See the Finish Line!

For Coaching Participants in The Lesson Program
Activity: Write down your assignment and due date!
1.
2.
3.
4.

Notes:

To Enroll, Scan the QR or visit KLETL.com

The Basics

Rise Above the Bully

So far in this book, we have focused a lot on personal development. The reason why I dedicated this entire book to personal development is those who are comfortable in their own skin and know themselves, are less likely to bully someone else. A key aspect of rising above the bully is to have and maintain a teachable personality.

A teachable personality is as simple as it sounds. You have to allow people to teach you. For you to be a great student, you have to understand and accept that you don't know everything. I know we live in a digital world where everything seems to be on the Internet, yet life is still done the old-fashioned way. Spending time on this earth will teach you a lot of things about people and yourself. It is important that you allow worthy people to speak into your life.

Not all voices that you hear you should pay attention to. If a person encourages you to perform beneath your potential, talks you out of positive thinking, or coaches you contrary to the "You, You want to become," you can omit their advice from your life. To operate a teachable personality, however, there are a few things you are willing to do. The biggest thing you are willing to do is "Listen."

A simple word, easy to spell, but how loaded of a word it is. You see, to listen correctly, you can't draw conclusions or strike down what a person is telling you without analyzing it. If someone wants to share something with you, listen, consider what they have said, and then make a choice on how you want to use that information.

If you are being corrected on how you do something or the way you think, listen to the advice. If it makes sense, keep it. If not, throw it away or store it for a rainy day. A teachable spirit has a willingness to get better. To be the best you, first, you must be willing to follow.

A lot of bullies are natural-born leaders. However, the key to being a great leader is to master controlling yourself. To lead people, you have to understand people and yourself and then how to bridge the gap. A leader encourages others to be their best and

The Lesson: Personal Development Author K. Lee strives to pull the best out of them. First, you have to push, motivate, and become great, and then you can lead others to greatness.

Self-control, in its simplest definition, means managing one's emotions, physical body, and thoughts. One thing self-control does not attempt to do is dominate and control others. I am not talking about a relationship of parent to child, but person to person. Until you can think for yourself and reason, a trustworthy person needs to make decisions for you. When you can understand and consider information, you are now able to control your being.

When you are in control, you are responsible for your choices, actions, and reactions. The key to making the best choices and actions and reacting appropriately to people whom you can't control is to control your response to them. We cannot make people do the right thing, but we can choose to do the right thing.

If someone tries to get you angry by making fun of you, cracking jokes, or telling lies about you. You have the choice to get angry and then decide if it is worth it. Consider if a person would believe the lies others told about you. Do you think they know you if they believe it? If they don't know you, is it worth choosing to fight with harsh words or physical action?

Of the many responses you can have, one response is better than others. Every action reacts, so if you do an action that deserves a reaction you don't want, choose to make a better choice. Notice that being angry is not a bad thing—in fact, it is normal. What

Rise Above the Bully

you want to do is channel your anger to prompt you to make the right decision. Fighting doesn't help anyone to win, but your reaction could save your life, give you time to do something else, and focus your attention on something better worth your time.

People are either distractions or help you achieve your end goal. Don't waste your time or emotions on people that are not worth it. Remember to listen to what people are saying and know that people who don't have your best interest at heart will lie to you. They will tell you the opposite of the truth in hopes you believe it.

They will tell you, "You are ugly," when you are "beautiful. Tell you, "You are dumb," when you're smart! Say you aren't worth nothing when a woman could have died to give birth to you, and she chose to give you life! You are special, you are important, you are somebody, you are beautiful, and you are smart. You are not living to your fullest potential if you believe these false sayings about you. Live life to the max and take control of yourself.

Transitioning to your thoughts, you must know the truth about you. You must know the areas you can improve, but never let anyone tell you you can't be better or you are a waste of time. If you are here on this earth, there is a purpose for you. A teachable spirit will keep you humble and allow you to accept healthy corrections that make you a better person.

Don't be a slave to your emotions, negative thoughts/thinking, or what your physical body may be

The Lesson: Personal Development Author K. Lee

tempted to do. Just because someone says something untrue about you doesn't mean you believe it. Just because a person may try to fight you doesn't mean you swing first. There are legal ramifications for such decisions, and no one wants to spend a moment of their time in juvenile.

When you are in control of yourself, you are free to love, be caring, practice patience, and build integrity. Yes, there are benefits to learning self-control. When you can manage your being, you can love others. Loving others begins with learning to love you. We are all worthy of love and should be respected.

The best form of loving others is to show that you are caring. We show that we care by seeking options that are good for everyone. Finding the right thing to do that benefits the majority, may not always be an easy decision but has to be made. If a person in your life or a friend is constantly in trouble, and you don't want to be, you need to have a conversation. A mutually beneficial choice is to talk to them about your desires and let them know that if they choose to continue to live that choice, you will not follow them.

You see, stopping friendships that are unhealthy for you is mutually beneficial. You cannot control what other people choose to do, but what you choose to do. By moving out of their way, you are allowing them to operate in their freedom to choose. You did your job of warning them of what would happen if they continued down that path, and now they had to choose.

The sad reality is that not everyone will choose

the right thing, even if it is the best thing to do. Don't allow yourself to be dragged down a downward spiral because you are trying to save someone. If appropriate, notify the right people who can help them and remove yourself so that you are not in a toxic situation.

If a person you know is choosing to do drugs, cut themself, steal, is a bulimic, or is practicing unhealthy habits, do tell someone who can help them, but don't feel obligated to save them. There are professionals who are certified, have the patience, and know how to help people with these habits. Let them do the work; your job is to let someone know who can help. A teacher can be the first step or telling their parent.

Chapter Recap!

To Rise Above, you must first learn to serve. Remember to listen to authority to learn the right way to do things. You can train others once you have mastered the right way of doing things! Before you become a great leader, you must first Master yourself! Take the time, do the work, and Pass The Lesson!

Great WORK!
Don't Stop Now, Two to Go!

For Coaching Participants in The Lesson Program
Activity: Write down your assignment and due date!
1.
2.
3.
4.

Notes:

To Enroll, Scan the QR or visit KLETL.com

Rise Above the Bully

Leadership 101

The previous chapter surely sets the foundation for Leadership 101. Every person is a natural-born leader because you always have at least one person to lead you! Leaders are people that are not focused on the numbers they lead but on the numbers they impact.

In life, you pass by several hundred thousand people in your lifetime, if not millions. I want you to take a second and jot down a few answers to the following questions: Are you living a life that leads you and others in the right direction? Are you fit to lead? Do you see the benefits of leadership? Do you have a model that is worth duplicating? Would you like to improve your skills as a leader?

Leadership 101

_____

_____

_____

_____

_____

_____

Let's take a closer look at those questions. Are you living a life that leads you and others in the right direction? Great leaders have self-control and self-confidence. You have to be certain that the decisions you make are ones you can stand by. In war and in life, the choices you make impact the people around you as well as yourself. When you make a choice, you want to be intentional.

What does that mean? A leader has to be responsible for the choices they make because they are responsible for themselves and those around them under their leadership. If you are at war, as a leader, the group is looking to you to make the decisions that best protect the team.

If you tell people to go or stand here, do this or that, you should have people set up to help support and protect each other. A true leader covers his people

The Lesson: Personal Development Author K. Lee

and is there to provide help. Would a parent/guardian make a decision that won't protect his/her child? They shouldn't. Every choice made should be based on preserving life.

Being a leader can be scary and it is tempting to want to shift blame when things go wrong or to shift control when you second-guess yourself. True leaders are not perfect, but they have a perfect heart to do good and that is what they do. A good leader has to value people, and themselves. Something not worth fighting for makes it very difficult to make great decisions.

You must decide that the people around you are worth fighting for. The choices you make, I make, we make impact the next generation. Many of you may choose to learn more about city government, and I encourage that. Serving your community and taking a leadership role is one of the best kinds of service to make social and legal changes.

Many leaders find out after their choices that they are leading others to greatness, and how great of a leader they are. Their choice to lead themselves to change had a ripple effect. Positive energy and choices attract positive outcomes. Sometimes, the outcome takes time, but it will show up. Don't quit doing the right thing because you may not see the benefit of your actions. Although the results may lag, good things are bound to come.

Are you fit to lead? Yes, of course you are! If you are willing to be taught how to be a better you, become the you, you want to be, and know your strengths and weaknesses, you are a great leader. A great leader doesn't know everything, nor are they capable of doing everything. They are a great resource for bringing talents together!

Think about it. You are a single person. How many resources do you have to bring together for your dreams to come to light? You have a teacher who helps you with academics, a coach who helps you with working out, a parent/guardian who helps you with nutrition and shelter, and you probably have other people like a pastor, counselor, or friends who help you learn other things.

All these people are coming together under your leadership because you control what you listen to and who your advisors are. You are calling the shots for how you process information. You are a natural-born leader, and yes, you are fit to lead. Leadership starts with you!

Do you see the benefits of leadership? The answer should be "yes!" All your choices have a cause and effect. Each semester, you are responsible for your work and are tested to either pass or fail. If you do the work, do the homework, and study for your exam, chances are you are going to earn a passing grade.

If you don't study for your test, choose not to do the work, don't come to class, and distract others in class with jokes. Don't be surprised if you earn a failing grade. Notice the keyword earn. As a leader, you can lead a life to greatness or destruction, and that choice

The Lesson: Personal Development Author K. Lee is up to the leader.

Do you have a model that is worth duplicating? Would you say your choices are ones more people should follow? Do you want to be the youth that sets an example that lifts your community? Will you be one that brings praise to your parents/guardians and those who love, care, and have invested in you? If there were a million more people like you, would that mean we could end poverty, help the homeless, eliminate debt, and/or stop bullying?

Or would that mean there would be war in the streets? Would the people be stealing from each other? No one could trust anyone because everyone turns on each other. Would the people say hateful things to each other and be a distraction for those who want to live a good life?

Are you a model worth duplicating? If that answer is not a yes, let's work on how we can make that answer a yes. Everyone desires and deserves to be celebrated for the great things they do for themselves and others. When you are a great model, people notice and ask, "How did you get to be so nice? So smart? So kind? So knowledgeable?" You can now give them an answer.

You can now point to the sources and people that help mold the leader you have become. Great leaders never toot their own horn, but they praise others; someday, someone will praise them. If you say you are great because of you and only you, you underestimate and devalue everyone around you. Everyone and

Leadership 101

everything around you can contribute to making you great or tearing you down. Know the difference and make wise choices to become the leader you were born to be.

Would you like to improve your skills as a leader? After you realize you are a leader, the learning process to become great will never stop. In life, there will always be someone who can teach you something. You want to maintain that teachable spirit and personality because that keeps you growing. The moment you shut yourself off for correction, information, or help, you stop your growth.

Don't ever get too old to where you can't remember to think as a child. A child is always open to listen and to learn. The one open to listening and learning will excel in every aspect of their life, from school to business. Listening and processing information is how you find solutions. If you have problems in your life, things are not going right, people are ignoring you, relationships are dying, It is time to listen.

Listening doesn't mean just hearing someone speak; it means keeping your heart and mind focused on what they're saying. Consider if what they're saying is true about you or a situation. Then you should decide what you are going to do about it.

Are you going to make the necessary changes? Will you offer apologies where they are due? Or try and fix what was broken? Will you opt out of everything and quit? Will you stop progress before it has a chance to grow?

The Lesson: Personal Development Author K. Lee

Don't be a quitter. Learn to start and finish everything you start. However, some things will come to an abrupt end. When you finish something, it could end because you have had a change of heart, and that is okay. Either way, finish it and move on to progress.

Don't get stuck in going in circles; make your decisions intentional. If the music you listen to, the movies you watch, and the people you hang around are horrible for your goals, make the responsible choice. Not everyone who calls you a friend is your friend; some are distractions and hindrances.

You don't have to maintain hurtful relationships. Instead, you owe it to yourself and to them to be free! We all have the freedom of choice. Never forget the power you have to choose what you will and won't do. Not every choice you make will be perfect, so you have to be open to change.

Leadership 101

Chapter Recap!

You are a natural-born leader. You can choose to lead to greatness or destruction. If you are duplicated a million times, will the world be greater, better, or worse? Depending on your answer, make changes or continue to grow to become an even better leader! Remember, take the time, do the work, and Pass The Lesson!

Great WORK!
Don't Stop Now, Just One to Go!

For Coaching Participants in The Lesson Program
Activity: Write down your assignment and due date!
1.
2.
3.
4.

Notes:

To Enroll, Scan the QR or visit KLETL.com

Leadership 101

The Lesson: Personal Development Author K. Lee

No One is Perfect

There is no such thing as a perfect family, leader, situation, or life. What we all have is a perfect opportunity to make something of ourselves by doing this: Appreciating your "Blended Family," learn about "Who You Are," become "Comfortable in Your Own Skin," don't be afraid to "Create the You, You Want to Be," get the right "Frame of Mind," master "The Basics," know you can "Rise Above the Bully," remember you have "Leadership 101" skills," and "No One is Perfect.

We all come from varied backgrounds. The diversity of our backgrounds should not be a division or repel us from pursuing the same dreams. We all desire the same things in life: to be great, to bless our families, and to impact our communities and the world prayerfully. If you come from a family that is wealthy, middle

No One is Perfect

class, or with financial difficulties, that doesn't change that desire. If your family has two dads or two moms, that doesn't change it. If you were/are being raised by a guardian, foster parent, or grandparent, that doesn't change it. If you are Black, Hispanic, Asian, or White, that doesn't change it either.

There is value in us all, and we are all able to positively contribute to our community, bless our families, and impact the world for the better. Don't ever think for a second that your background has to determine your future. You now know who you are; if you don't, I am sure you have a stronger idea. When you start the journey to learn about who you are, the journey will continue for the rest of your life because you mature and grow year after year.

Never stop being willing to grow and learn to be comfortable within your own skin. You may not have the hair you want, the body you want, the grades you want; but decide to make changes to get you there and be comfortable with your work in progress. Nothing goes from zero to a hundred. A plant starts from a seed, then a bud, then a stem, then a leaf, a flower, then maybe a bush, and lastly, a tree.

The best benefits in life are the journey and not just the outcome. The ends don't justify the means. Greatness is not by any means necessary but by the right choices we make. The means, the choices, won't justify the end. The wise turtle, slow and steady, beat out the quick and unfocused hare. Stay focused on the you, you want to become.

The Lesson: Personal Development Author K. Lee

If you have to create a vision board, create a collage, make a book, write a story, sing a song, design a budget, create a website! Do what you need to stay focused. Find the mentors you need to get from where you are to where you want to be. Don't be afraid to pick up a book. Ask a librarian what sections to go to. It is amazing how many people never ask a librarian any questions, and they have such a wealth of information!

As you make the right changes and locate the right mentors, remember to have the right frame of mind. Don't be offended if you have to make changes in your life. If you have to remove harmful friends, do it. If you can't hang out with them because they steal, drink, or smoke, and you don't, don't feel bad. Remove toxic people and thinking from your mindset.

It may seem hard to do at first, but over time, it gets easier. It is a little different with family because your family will ideally be around. In these cases, you just have to communicate what you will and won't do. If they don't respect your choices, communicate that to an adult, and remove yourself from situations and events that tempt you to do bad things.

In life, you have to learn the basics so you can be entrusted to have more freedom. When you master the basics, you can be trusted to cook for yourself and potentially be left at home alone because your parent/guardian knows you are responsible. If you can't be trusted because you don't do the basics, you can't be mad if you don't have the responsibility.

No One is Perfect

As you prove yourself by following directions, making your bed, doing your homework, and doing well with your chores, you will find people don't mind doing things for you. I remember when I was a kid, my older sister always cleaned up, made great grades, and constantly got new shoes, clothes, and stuff she wanted. My siblings and I started doing better with our chores because we wanted what she had. If you see someone with something you want, don't steal, fight, or pull them down. Ask them how they got it! Then, do the work to earn it.

Learning these many techniques will make you a confident person. A confident, self-controlled person does not want to control everyone else because they are busy controlling themselves. Rising above the bully means you are open to the differences other people introduce to your life. You don't have to agree with everything other people choose to do, but you can choose to respect their freedom of choice.

When we learn to respect others and respect ourselves, we fight the urge to be a bully. The only thing worse than a young bully is an adult bully, sometimes described as a tyrant, bigot, intolerant, manipulative, conniving, demoralizing, self-hating, prideful, and more.

Don't take these nasty characteristics into your character description. All balanced people are not so easily bothered by the thoughts and actions of others. They are more concerned about their thoughts, actions, and reactions because they know those choices affect everyone. You are a leader, so don't hesitate to

The Lesson: Personal Development Author K. Lee

leverage your authority.

Leadership 101 starts with leading your own life. You want to lead a life that first makes you happy, benefits those around you, and leads to a better tomorrow. If your choices cancel out options for you and deny you rights and responsibility, I check your leadership model. You want to create a model others want to duplicate for their betterment.

Many of you may choose to own a business, get a job, have a family, and if so, you want to lead them to greatness and not failure. The choices you make now are laying the foundation for where you can lead them. Never get to a point where you think you can't benefit from listening to someone else. There is always room to grow.

The best leaders understand they can never be perfect, but they strive for perfection. You want to make the right choices because they impact everyone around you, present and future. That sounds like a loaded responsibility, but you take it like you would eat an elephant—one bite and day at a time. Remember, no one is perfect.

It ought to be a breath of fresh air to know that no one is perfect, no matter how perfect they look. We all have flaws, and you can make all the right decisions, but still, things are out of your control or may not go as planned. Don't panic, and remember to take the good with the bad. Remember to enjoy life and stay positive. Positive energy attracts positive things.

No One is Perfect

I am super proud that you've completed this book! Yup, there are no more chapters after this if you don't want to read the About the Author. Remember, you are a leader; you are important, amazing, and uniquely made. Don't allow anyone or anything to convince you otherwise.

Chapter Recap!

Keep this book, and remember to use it as often as needed! Some books you can grow with and find you keep using time after time. Recommend this book to your friends, and be sure to catch the next book in the series coming out soon. Congratulations, you took the time, did the work, and Passed The Lesson!

Great WORK!
Go Out, Lead your Life to Greatness, and Impact the World for the Greater!

For Coaching Participants in The Lesson Program
Activity: Write down your assignment and due date!
1.
2.
3.
4.

Notes:

To Enroll, Scan the QR or visit KLETL.com

No One is Perfect

About The Author

"God blesses those who work for peace, for they will be called the children of God." Matthew 5:9

Krystal Lee is proud to have authored this book and accompanying course to better the lives of readers. She has a heart to help people in their deepest times of need. She writes because she believes there is power in sharing stories and life accounts, that others can benefit and learn from. Sharing is caring, so she shares stories, ideas, and resources to better the lives of her readers.

In addition, Dr. Lee has authored over 20 books across seven or more genres (adult, children, youth fiction, self-help, spiritual growth, novels, and more), in addition to ghostwriting and editing more than 15 published works. She has launched coaching programs, web courses, and helped in the formulation of many startup companies. Her specialty lies in aiding coaches, creatives, and service-based companies in defining their message, brand, unique selling point, client avatar, and generating a sales cycle and structure for her clients.

Empowering individuals is at the core of her work, and she is driven by her passion to continue writing. In addition to being an author, Krystal Lee is a business owner of multiple companies, a consultant, an ordained chaplain, and a speaker.

For more information about Dr. Krystal Lee or to engage with her further, please scan the provided QR code. To engage with the Coaching series and Monthly Meet up Group for Embrace Your Crown First Sundays at 4pm, please use the QR code or visit KLEembrace.com

ENGAGE
LEARN MORE

Shop Books from AuthorKLee.com

Explore over seven different book genres, and find something suitable for every member of the family.

Scan to Shop All Titles by K. Lee

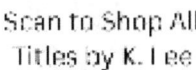
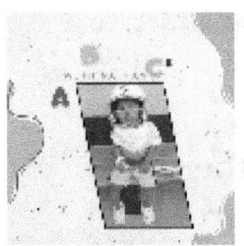

It's time to start and finish **YOUR Story**!

KLE Publishing specializes in helping people become authors. In as little as 15 to 90 days, we can help you develop your book and publish to 39,000 outlets!

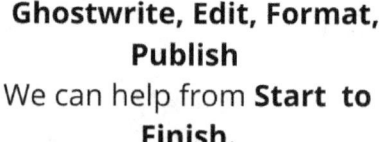

Ghostwrite, Edit, Format, Publish
We can help from **Start to Finish.**

Scan and fill out the short form to learn more and connect with us.

KLEPub.com Authors

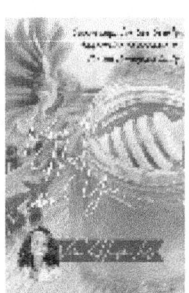
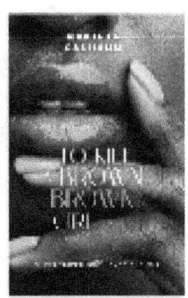

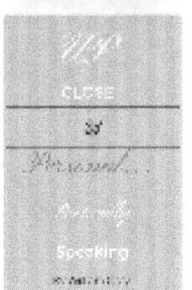

www.ingramcontent.com/pod-product-compliance
Lightning Source LLC
Chambersburg PA
CBHW070630300426
44113CB00010B/1719